The Bombing of London 2005

Andrew Langley

www.raintreepublishers.co.uk
Visit our website to find out more information about **Raintree** books.

To order:
☎ Phone 44 (0) 1865 888112
▤ Send a fax to 44 (0) 1865 314091
▢ Visit the Raintree Bookshop at www.raintreepublishers.co.uk to browse our catalogue and order online.

First published in Great Britain by Raintree, Halley Court, Jordan Hill, Oxford OX2 8EJ, part of Harcourt Education. Raintree is a registered trademark of Harcourt Education Ltd.

© Harcourt Education Ltd 2006

Editorial: Richard Woodham and Andrew Farrow
Design: David Poole
Illustrations: Geoff Ward
Picture Research: Maria Joannou and Catherine Bevan
Production: Chloe Bloom

Originated by Chroma Graphics
Printed and bound in Hong Kong, China by South China Printing Company

10 digit ISBN 1 406 20438 2
13 digit ISBN 978 1 4062 0438 4

10 09 08 07 06
10 9 8 7 6 5 4 3 2 1

British Library Cataloguing in Publication Data
Langley, Andrew
The Bombing of London 2005
363.3'25'09421
A full catalogue record for this book is available from the British Library.

Acknowledgements
The publishers would like to thank the following for permission to reproduce photographs:
Corbis pp. **13** (ABC News/Reuters), **19** (Tim Hawkins/Eye Ubiquitous), **21** (Reuters/David Parry/Newscast/Handout), **39** (Sion Touhig), **40** (Menezes family/Reuters); Empics pp. **7** (PA/Metropolitan Police), **11** (AP/Alexander Chadwick), **23** (Metropolitan Police), **25** (AP/Lefteris Pitarakis), **29** (AP/Matt Dunham), **37** (PA/John Giles), **45** (AP Photo); Getty Images pp. **5** (Photographers Choice), **15** (AFP/ Joshua Roberts); Reuters p. **43** (Paul Hackett); Rex Features pp. **17** (Eddie Mulholland), **26** (Tamara Beckwith), **31** (Alisdair Macdonald), **33**, **35** (Richard Crampton), **47** (Ray Tang).

Cover image of Davinia Turrell being led away from Edgware Road tube station by Paul Dadge, reproduced with permission of Rex Features (HXL).

The publishers would like to thank Dr Fiona Stephen for her assistance in the preparation of this book.

Every effort has been made to contact copyright holders of any material reproduced in this book. Any omissions will be rectified in subsequent printings if notice is given to the publishers.

The paper used to print this book comes from sustainable resources.

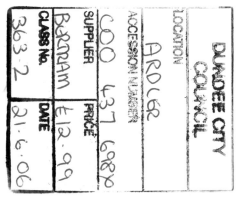

Contents

Any words appearing in the text in bold, **like this**, are explained in the glossary.

"I thought that was it when it all went so dark."

1
Bombs underground

An ordinary day

Every weekday, more than 3 million people travel to work in London. About 750,000 of these come from towns and villages outside London. Some travel by road, some by railway. Some cycle and some walk. Most of them use buses or underground trains.

Thursday 7 July 2005 began just like an ordinary day. Workers made their usual journeys in the **rush hour** to the centre of London. It was the middle of summer and the weather was fine and dry.

London was in the news. The day before, the city had been chosen to host the 2012 Olympic Games. There had been huge celebrations and many Londoners felt proud and excited. Now life seemed to be back to normal. But this Thursday was going to be far from normal. It was about to turn into one of the most tragic and frightening days in London's history.

Millions of people travel into London every weekday morning.

Leeds to London

Early that morning, while it was still dark, three men left their homes in West Yorkshire. They were heading for central London. Climbing into a hired car, they set off southwards at about 4:00 a.m. There were also several rucksacks in the car, packed with high explosives and **detonators**.

All three men had been born and educated in Britain. The youngest was 18-year-old Hasib Hussain, who had spent all his life in the Holbeck area of Leeds. His friend, 22-year-old Shehzad Tanweer, lived nearby. He was a quiet and religious person, interested in cricket and martial arts. Mohammed Sidique Khan was 30. He had worked as a teaching assistant at a Leeds primary school for three years.

London travel facts

- Weekday trips in central London:
  bus 4.6 million
  underground train 2.7 million
  car, taxi, or other vehicle 11.0 million

- There are 275 London Underground stations and 12 underground lines.

- There are 649 bus routes in London (more than any other city in Europe), served by over 6,800 buses.

- Between 7:00 and 10:00 a.m. on weekdays, more than 1 million people enter central London.

- At these peak times over 500 train services operate.

2004–05 figures

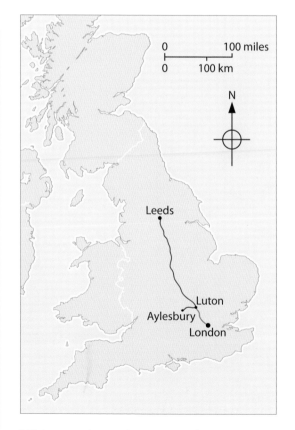

This map shows the routes taken by the four bombers.

This image, taken by a security camera, shows the four bombers entering Luton station at 7:21 a.m.

The three men ended their long road journey at Luton, just outside London. At 6:51 a.m. they parked the car outside Luton railway station, where they met a fourth man. Germaine Lindsay, 19, had also spent time in Yorkshire but now lived in Aylesbury, Buckinghamshire, with his wife and baby. He had also reached Luton by car. The four men then walked together into the station and took a train to King's Cross station in London. Each man carried a rucksack on his back.

After leaving the train at King's Cross, the men walked to the underground railway station. There they split up, each one going a different way. Shehzad Tanweer boarded a Circle Line underground train, heading east. Mohammed Sidique Khan took a Circle Line train in the opposite direction, heading west. Germaine Lindsay went south on the Piccadilly Line. It was rush hour and all the trains were full of people.

Hasib Hussain was supposed to go north, on the Northern Line. But when he reached the platform he found that the trains on that line were delayed because of a fault with the signalling system. Police believe he decided to head for north London anyway, and walked along the road towards Euston station looking for a bus.

The first blasts

Tanweer, Sidique Khan, and Lindsay were now on board three trains and moving into the underground tunnels. At 8:50 a.m. each of them pressed a button or switch in their rucksacks. Within 50 seconds of each other, all three of the bombs exploded.

Germaine Lindsay was in a Piccadilly Line train travelling from King's Cross to Russell Square. He was sitting or standing near the front set of doors in the first carriage. When the bomb detonated, there was a loud bang. The train suddenly stopped and all the lights went out. The carriages quickly filled up with sooty, black smoke.

❝ The train just stopped and then all of a sudden it just filled with gassy smoke. You couldn't breathe and it was stinging our eyes. It was very scary. We thought we weren't going to get out, because we couldn't get off the train. ❞

Christina Lawrence, Russell Square

Mohammed Sidique Khan was in a Circle Line train over two miles away. It had just pulled out of Edgware Road station and was heading for Paddington. He had put his rucksack on the floor of the second carriage. The explosion caused a large flash of light and a bang. The train halted and the lights went out. Dust and soot filled the air.

Shehzad Tanweer was in a Circle Line train going east from Liverpool Street towards Aldgate station. He had also put his rucksack on the floor, at the back of the second carriage. The bomb went off with an enormous bang. It tore away part of the roof and sent out a shower of glass fragments from the windows.

> **❝** I was being twisted and thrown to the ground. I thought I wasn't going to get out of this – whatever it was – I just didn't know. I thought that was it when it all went so dark. Then I touched my hand to my face and felt the blood and knew it wasn't all over yet. **❞**
>
> Michael Henning, Liverpool Street

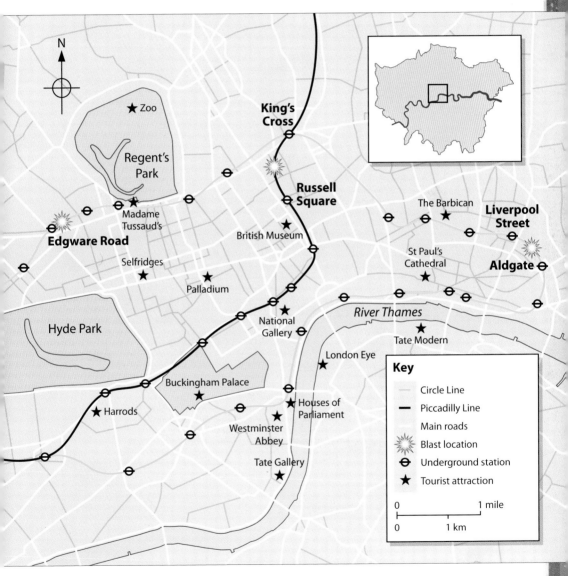

This map shows the locations of the three underground bombs. **❙**

2
Escape from horror

The first reactions

Up at ground level, nobody knew exactly what had happened. There were reports of explosions or loud bangs in the tunnels. Some people thought that two trains had collided. The operators of the underground system had not heard the explosions. All they knew was that the trains had stopped. At first they thought this was due to a sudden **power surge**, and that too much electricity had made the system shut down.

In the tunnels below, there was confusion and terror. Passengers on all three trains were stunned with shock. They were packed together in the darkness and surrounded by thick, black smoke. It was hard to breathe and people covered their noses with handkerchiefs and tissues. Many people were wounded, and some were dead. The survivors had just one aim – to get out of the choking darkness and up to fresh air and safety.

This picture was taken using a mobile phone camera. It shows passengers evacuating the bombed train near Russell Square.

Panic and calm

In the train near Russell Square, there was a moment of panic. Some people started screaming and crying, and several tried to break the windows to let in air. But most passengers stayed calm. Emergency lights came on in the tunnel. The driver told everyone to stay where they were. He had to make sure that the electric current to the **live rail** had been switched off before anyone got down from the train.

The scene near Edgware Road was just as terrifying. There were screams and cries for help from those who were injured or trapped. Several people lay wounded or dead on the floor of the second carriage. Many others had blood on their faces and ripped clothes. Some passengers tried to force open the sliding doors, but soon gave up. The driver came through from his cabin to announce that help was on the way.

Some passengers in the bombed train near Liverpool Street thought it had come off the rails. People tried to smash the windows with fire extinguishers, but this made the carriages rock and caused more alarm. Most people were in a state of shock.

After about 20 minutes, help arrived. London Underground staff cleared away some of the debris from the explosions and then opened the doors of the trains. They calmed the passengers and began giving first aid to the wounded. The police and emergency services reached the trains about 30 minutes after the blasts.

The survivors climbed down from the carriages. Outside the train, the air was clearer and they could breathe more easily. They walked along the tunnels to the nearest platform, guided by Underground staff. Passengers on the Liverpool Street train only had about 100 metres to go. They were led down the track past the carriage where the bomb had exploded and blown off the roof. There were bodies on the ground nearby.

ABC News Exclusive

This photo shows the damage caused by the bomb that exploded near Edgware Road station.

Casualties underground

Piccadilly Line train between King's Cross and Russell Square:
26 dead, unknown injured

Circle Line train between Edgware Road and Paddington:
7 dead, about 120 injured

Circle Line train between Liverpool Street and Aldgate:
7 dead, at least 100 injured

The first reports

Many people on ground level had heard the noise of the explosions. Shopkeepers near Aldgate station had felt their buildings shake and heard the windows rattle. Very soon afterwards smoke could be seen coming from the station entrance. Then the first passengers from the trains appeared, many of them wounded or stained with smoke.

At Edgware Road station, Underground staff lined the way as the passengers walked along the tunnel and up on to the platform. Then at last they were on the street. "I cannot tell you how happy I was to see the sky," said one survivor. There was a branch of Marks & Spencer near the station entrance. The passengers were led into the store and given basic first aid and water.

The early reports about the bombings were very confused. Police thought at first that there were five explosions. This was because two of the blasts occurred between stations. Some survivors escaped from the front of the trains, others from the rear. As a result, passengers emerged at five different stations.

TERRORISM AND 9/11

On 11 September 2001 (a day now known as "9/11"), **Islamic extremists** took control of four airliners over the USA. They crashed two of them into the twin towers of the World Trade Center in New York, which collapsed. Another plane hit the **Pentagon** in Washington, and a fourth crashed into a field. Nearly 3,000 people were killed altogether. These tragic events caused many Western governments to make their security systems stronger, in case they too were attacked.

Streets were closed to allow the emergency services to reach the scene quickly.

It took nearly an hour for the police to get a clearer picture of what had happened. Only now did they learn that there had been three explosions, and that they had gone off at the same time. The most important thing now was to take control of the streets so that fire engines, ambulances, and other emergency services could get through to the scene.

The police were well prepared. Since the attack on the World Trade Center in New York in 2001, the British government had expected a similar incident in London. The army, the police, and other services had carefully practised what to do in such a crisis. Now they put their emergency plan into operation. By 9:49 a.m. the entire London Underground system had been shut down. Trains were halted in the stations and all services were stopped. Many streets in central London were closed to ordinary traffic.

Searching for a target

Meanwhile Hasib Hussain had reached the approach to Euston station, about 800 metres west of King's Cross. It was now about 30 minutes since the explosions on the trains. The Underground network was starting to close down and passengers were being **evacuated** from stations. The Euston Road was full of people looking for another way to get to work.

Hussain was still searching for a new target for his bomb. He had tried to contact the other bombers on his mobile phone, but had got no answer. They were already lying dead in the wreckage of three Tube trains. Hussain decided to go to North London. He joined the queue for the number 30 bus, which was going to an area of London called Hackney Wick.

The bus arrived at Euston at 9:35 a.m. Hussain got on board and climbed to the upper deck, where he took a seat at the back. Because some roads had been closed after the earlier bombings, the bus could not use its normal route. By 9:47 a.m. it had turned south through Tavistock Square. Hussain pressed the switch which detonated his bomb.

There was a gigantic boom, and fragments of glass and metal flew everywhere. The explosion destroyed the back part of the top deck and ripped off the roof. It also forced the floor down, crushing people below. People sitting at the front of the bus survived, but 14 people in the rear were killed and many others were injured. Among the dead was Hasib Hussain.

❝ We heard an explosion – something like a big bang, sort of muffled inside a metal container. We looked back and saw a huge metal scrap thing on the road, with a few fumes coming out… All of us panicked and hurried to get out of the bus… This was the first time I smelt death so near. **❞**

Krishnakumar Nair , Tavistock Square

Early morning, 7 July 2005

4:00 a.m.	Mohammed Sidique Khan, Hasib Hussain, and Shehzad Tanweer leave Leeds by car
5:00 a.m.	Germaine Lindsay arrives by car at Luton station
6:51 a.m.	The three other bombers arrive at Luton station
8:30 a.m.	The four men get off a train at King's Cross station
8:50 a.m.	Three bombs explode on underground trains
9:19 a.m.	Police issue **terrorist alert**; London Underground begins closing down its system
9:35 a.m.	Hasib Hussain boards a number 30 bus outside Euston station
9:47 a.m.	Bomb explodes on the bus in Tavistock Square (*see map*)

King's Cross

Russell Square

Tavistock Square

British Museum

The fourth bomb was so powerful that most of the top half of the bus was destroyed.

"Whatever you do, however many you kill, you will fail."

3
Searching for survivors

Treating the wounded

The fourth explosion increased the confusion in the central London streets. What was happening? Why were roads and railways being shut down? People could not even use their mobile phones to get information, because the networks were not working. But slowly the situation became clearer. At 10:00 a.m. the **National Grid** announced that there had not been any power surges on the Underground. Many now realized that the explosions must have been caused by bombs.

Now the most urgent aim was to look after the survivors. At least 700 people had been wounded, and all of them needed medical treatment. Some of them were still trapped underground. Doctors, nurses, and the ambulance service rushed into action, but they were going to be stretched to the limit. Hospitals had to call in staff who were on holiday or off duty, as well as extra doctors from as far away as Hampshire and Oxfordshire.

The air ambulance was used to bring doctors to the scenes of the explosions.

A medical emergency

The emergency services began to arrive at the scenes of the first explosions at about 9:20 a.m. Several specialist doctors travelled straight to the sites from their hospitals by air ambulance helicopters. By this time hundreds of passengers from the damaged trains had reached the station entrances. Most were shocked and distressed, but many were wounded. At least 90 injured people emerged from Aldgate station alone.

As quickly as possible, medical workers treated the most urgent cases. The ticket hall and waiting rooms at King's Cross station were turned into a temporary hospital for people hurt in the Piccadilly Line bombing. Doctors also performed emergency operations on the concourse of Liverpool Street station.

The explosion on the number 30 bus took place outside the headquarters of the British Medical Association. At the time, many doctors were attending courses and conferences there. They immediately rushed from the building to help the wounded passengers.

Medical staff were able to give on-the-spot treatment to about half of the 700 people injured in the four incidents. The rest (more than 350) were more seriously wounded, and had to be transferred to hospital. There were not enough ambulances to move all the patients, so buses were used to transport those who were able to walk.

Victims of all nations

The 7 July bombings were not just a British tragedy. Among the 56 who died were people from Italy, Turkey, Poland, Iran, Nigeria, Mauritius, Australia, Israel, and Sri Lanka. Many of the injured were also foreign nationals, including visitors from South Africa, Sierra Leone, Colombia, New Zealand, and China.

The streets had to be kept clear so that emergency vehicles could get through. At 11:08 a.m. bus services in central London were closed down. The police asked people in London to stay where they were – at home, at work, or in schools. They also advised them not to travel in the centre if possible, and not to call the emergency services.

Most of the serious injury cases were taken to the Royal London Hospital at Mile End, in the east of the city. Operations involved removing fragments of metal or glass and repairing broken or gashed limbs. Twenty-two of these people were in a very bad condition, and one person died later that night in the hospital.

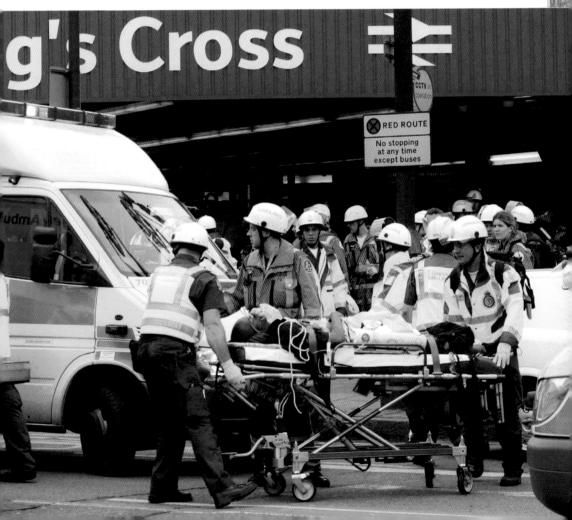

Ambulances transported many of the injured to nearby hospitals.

Down in the wreckage

After the wounded had been evacuated from the tunnels, the search began for the dead. Teams from the London Fire Brigade made sure that there was nothing burning. There were also checks to find out whether the bombs had contained any dangerous chemical or **biological agents**, such as **nerve gas**. Once all was clear, the paramedics entered the tunnels.

Conditions underground were still horrible. Worst of all was the scene near King's Cross, on the Piccadilly Line. The train had been in a narrow tunnel when the bomb exploded. The narrow space had made the **impact** of the bomb more powerful than in the wider, double-track tunnels on the Circle Line. The explosion had badly damaged the brickwork of the walls and roof. Workers had to support them with timber and metal props to stop them collapsing.

There were other dangers. The air was very hot and filled with fumes and dust, as well as the dangerous fibres from **asbestos** sheeting. People could only work for short periods in the heat. The tunnel was also home to hundreds of rats, whose bite can pass on serious diseases. Workers also had to force their way through the wreckage of the train before they could reach the bodies. Up above, special **refrigerated trucks** waited to take away the corpses.

Deep and narrow

The Piccadilly Line is one of the deepest underground railways in London. It runs through tunnels which are 30 metres deep in places – four times deeper than the Circle Line. The tunnels are also only 3.5 metres wide. The tunnel ceiling is so low that the roof of a train passes just 15 centimetres underneath it.

At the same time, the police investigation started. Officers hung **security curtains** over the entrances to the bombed Tube stations, and screened off the site of the wrecked bus. Members of the Anti-Terrorist Branch of the Metropolitan Police went down into the tunnel and began the painstaking job of looking for clues about the bombers. Every fragment of glass, metal, and plastic had to be examined carefully. It was going to take a very long time.

The Circle Line explosions scattered evidence over a wide area of track.

Out of touch

The bombings had brought death and injury for hundreds of people. They had also caused panic and bewilderment for thousands more. Across the city, Londoners found that they could hardly move. Blocked roads and closed transport systems meant that getting to work or school was nearly impossible. The police told everyone in the centre to stay where they were.

By the evening, things were not much better. Getting home again was very difficult, and many people found the only way to reach their houses was to walk. In the confusion, many lost touch with their friends and families. The mobile phone network was still not working, so they could not talk to each other. The public now knew that several people had been killed in the explosions, although nobody knew any details about them.

Hundreds of missing persons posters were put up in London in the days after the bombings.

Lost and found

Martine Wright disappeared on the day of the bombings. For two days her family and boyfriend searched the hospitals and streets. Around 36 hours after the explosions, they found her in a hospital. She had suffered terrible injuries, including the loss of both legs, but she was alive.

Benedetta Ciaccia was last heard from at 7:00 a.m. on 7 July. After many hours of searching, it was discovered that she had died in the explosion near Liverpool Street.

Many travellers did not get home that night. Some seemed simply to have vanished. They had set out for work but had never arrived. Something had happened to them on their journey. Perhaps they had been caught up in the attacks? Were they dead, or trapped in the tunnels, or lying injured in a hospital bed?

Relatives and friends of the missing began a desperate search. Throughout the night and the next day they went from hospital to hospital trying to track down lost children, parents, friends, or partners. They put up posters and handed out photographs of the missing to people in the street, in the hope that someone might recognize them and know where they were.

4
Who did it?

A claim is made

At 11:10 a.m., within two hours of the blasts, the chief of the London Metropolitan Police made a statement to the press. He revealed that his officers had found evidence of explosives at one of the sites. This meant, he said, that the incidents were "probably a major terrorist attack", but he did not know for certain who was responsible. At 12:05 p.m., the Prime Minister, Tony Blair, called them "barbaric" terrorist attacks.

Then, at 12:15 p.m., a statement appeared on an Islamic extremist website. It claimed that the bombings had been carried out by a terrorist group named "Secret Organization – al-Qaeda in Europe". This was what many people in London had already suspected. They had been warned many times that attacks like this would take place.

After the blasts

9:49 a.m.	London Underground system shut down
11:08 a.m.	Bus services in central London shut down
11:10 a.m.	Metropolitan Police Commissioner Ian Blair confirms that there are traces of explosives at the sites, showing that this is a terrorist incident
12:05 p.m.	Prime Minister Tony Blair condemns "barbaric" attacks
12:15 p.m.	A little-known group called "Secret Organization – al-Qaeda in Europe" claims in a website message that it carried out the bombings
3:26 p.m.	Deputy Metropolitan Police chief Brian Paddick confirms that police had no warning of the attacks
4:30 p.m.	Services resume on most mainline railways in London
5:30 p.m.	Tony Blair returns to London from Scotland and makes a statement outside 10 Downing Street
6:15 p.m.	Police confirm that at least 37 people have died in the blasts

Al-Qaeda is a network of Islamic extremists whose aim is to bring terror to countries it believes are hostile to **Islam**. Its most infamous act is the destruction of the World Trade Center in New York on 11 September 2001. Since then, al-Qaeda had declared that Britain was also a terrorist target, because British troops had taken part in the invasion of Iraq in 2003.

Al-Qaeda was responsible for the destruction of the World Trade Center on 11 September 2001.

The morning after

Friday 8 July was another working day, but the centre of London was strangely quiet. Many people stayed away, either because their workplaces were still closed or because they were afraid to travel. Ten of the city's twelve Underground lines had reopened, although three of them had limited services. Many **commuters** chose to travel by taxi, which seemed safer. Buses, which were normally packed during the rush hour, were now less than half full.

There was still a feeling of danger in the air. Armed police officers patrolled the stations and main streets. Most people now believed that the explosions had been caused by Islamic extremist **suicide bombers**. Many people were afraid that more explosions were planned. Travellers studied their fellow passengers nervously, especially anyone who carried a rucksack, or was of Middle-Eastern origin.

Meanwhile the police were trying to work out what had happened. Forensics experts were combing the blast sites inch by inch, examining every fragment for clues. They already knew that the first three bombs had gone off at almost exactly the same moment, and had all been placed on the floor near the carriage doors.

Had they been detonated by one person from some distance away, by using the signal from a mobile phone? This had happened in the terrorist bombings in Madrid, Spain, in 2004. Police did not think so, because mobile signals are difficult to pick up in the deep tunnels of the London Underground. All this showed that the attacks must have been carried out by more than one terrorist.

It was the beginning of the biggest manhunt the United Kingdom had ever seen. At this stage, the police did not know for certain that all four bombers were dead. The police had to search for anyone who might have been involved, either as leader, organizer, or bomb-maker. The chief of the Metropolitan Police asked members of the public for help. "We're appealing to anyone who knows anything," he said. Any information might be useful, even if it had not seemed important at the time.

Many commuters chose not to travel on the Underground on the day after the bombings.

London struggles back after bombings.

ABC News, 8 July 2005

The Madrid bombings

On 11 March 2004, Islamic extremists struck in Madrid, the capital of Spain. Ten explosions on four trains during the morning rush hour killed 191 people and wounded around 1,500. The terrorists were eventually cornered south of the city, but they blew themselves up before they could be captured.

The response at home

British leaders quickly spoke out against the bombings. Prime Minister Tony Blair left an important meeting with world leaders in Edinburgh to return to London for a crisis meeting with his security chiefs. He urged the public not to be terrorized. Queen Elizabeth II visited victims of the attacks in the Royal London Hospital. She later said, "Those who perpetrate these brutal acts against innocent people should know that they will not change our way of life."

Ordinary people made their own statements defying the terrorists. For example, a website was set up inviting people to post photographs of themselves holding up a sign saying "We are not afraid". Soon the site was receiving messages from all over the world. Many Londoners also left flowers and cards for the victims near the bombed sites. One card read, "Yesterday we fled this great city, but today we are walking back into an even stronger, greater city."

Messages of support came from leaders in all parts of the world. The Secretary-General of the United Nations Organization, Kofi Annan, described the bombings as "an attack on humanity itself". The President of the United States, George Bush, expressed his "heartfelt" sorrow in a conversation with Tony Blair. A Chinese spokesman said that China was shocked by the tragedy. Countries as far apart as South Africa, Australia, and Iceland joined to condemn the terrorists.

The vast majority of Muslims also made clear that they were horrified. Religious scholars in Saudi Arabia, Lebanon, and Egypt stated that the murderous attacks were crimes which could not be justified by any religion – and certainly not Islam. A Palestinian leader of the Islamic organization Hamas said that he "denounced and rejected" the slaughter of innocent civilians.

This memorial service for victims of the bombings was held on 14 July, a week after the explosions.

66 [People] choose to come to London, as so many have come before, because they come to be free, they come to live the life they choose, they come to be able to be themselves. They flee you because you tell them how they should live. They don't want that, and nothing you do, however many of us you kill, will stop that flight to our city where freedom is strong and where people can live in harmony with one another. Whatever you do, however many you kill, you will fail. **99**

Ken Livingstone, Mayor of London, 7 July 2005

Breakthrough

The first major breakthrough came the day after the explosions. The mother of Hasib Hussain reported that he was missing. He had told his family that he was going on a day trip to London, but no one had heard from him since. Police officers soon found evidence that a person matching Hussain's description had been on the bombed bus in Tavistock Square. Police could also tell that he had been sitting near to where the bomb had exploded.

In the days that followed, the picture became clearer. The police began to examine over 2,500 items. These included **CCTV** footage from **security cameras** at all nearby railway stations and public places, and evidence picked up from the blast sites. CCTV footage showed Hussain talking with three other men at King's Cross station shortly before the explosions. All four men were carrying rucksacks. The bodies of the four men, together with identification, were found at the four blast sites.

On 12 July, the police had enough proof to take a major step forward. They raided 6 houses in the Leeds area. Among them were Hussain's family home in Holbeck, the nearby home of his friend Shehzad Tanweer, and two properties belonging to Mohammed Sidique Khan in Dewsbury. They also sealed off the area near a house in Burley after they found a large quantity of explosives there. About 500 people had to be evacuated from the neighbourhood.

Further south, the police had narrowed their hunt to Luton. CCTV footage showed the four men entering the railway station on the day of the bombings. Soon afterwards officers found the hire car used by the bombers, still in the car park. The station was closed as they carefully examined the vehicle. Under the front seat was another rucksack containing two bombs, both made by stuffing explosives and nails into glass bottles. A day later, on 13 July, police raided the home of Germaine Lindsay in nearby Aylesbury.

CCTV footage from King's Cross station showed Hussain, right, leaving a shop before boarding the bus.

YORKS ARREST LINKED TO LONDON BOMBINGS

Police have evidence linking four men – including three from West Yorkshire – to the scenes of last week's London bombings, detectives have said. This morning anti-terror police searched six properties in the Leeds area and arrested one man... The driving licence and cash card of one suspect, who was 19 and from Leeds, were found in the mangled wreckage of the number 30 bus which blew up in Tavistock Square.

Daily Telegraph, 12 July 2005

The police search

The first 3 months of the investigation involved:

- watching 80,000 CCTV tapes
- taking more than 3,000 written statements from witnesses
- searching 15 different locations
- seizing 30,000 items, including 1,000 from a flat in Leeds
- sifting through a landfill site in West Yorkshire.

Going worldwide

On 14 July, exactly one week after the attack, people throughout Britain took part in a 2-minute silence. Wherever they were, at work or school or home, they stood quiet and still in memory of the victims. The number of dead was now known to be 52, although others were still thought to be missing.

Four of the dead were the bombers themselves. But had anybody else been involved in the plot? Had the bombs left in the car been meant for other bombers? The police announced that they wanted to question several other people. Among them was an Egyptian chemistry lecturer called Magdi Asdi el-Nashar, who had been living in Leeds. Shortly before the bombings, he returned to Cairo. He was arrested there but denied that he had any link with the plot.

On 17 July the families of three of the suicide bombers issued statements to the press. They described their shock when they heard that their relatives had taken part in the attacks. Other people who knew them were also amazed. "He was a good man, quiet," said a parent at the school where Mohammad Sidique Khan worked. Shehzad Tanweer's uncle described his nephew as "a very kind and calm person".

But as the police dug deeper into the background of the four men, a different picture began to emerge. Hasib Hussain had visited relatives in Pakistan in 2003. There he had become devoutly religious. In November 2004, Khan and Tanweer had also spent time in Pakistan. Nobody knew exactly what they had been doing there, but some believe they might have attended courses taught by Islamic extremists.

❝ Islam strictly, strongly and severely condemns the use of violence and the destruction of innocent lives. Suicide bombings, which killed and injured innocent people in London, are *haram*, – vehemently prohibited in Islam, and those who committed these barbaric acts are criminals not martyrs.

The Holy **Qu'ran** declares: "Whoever kills a human being… then it is as though he has killed all mankind." **❞**

A fatwa (religious decree) issued by the British Muslim Forum on 18 July 2005

The police raided many houses in connection with the bombings.

There was also a possible link between the bombers and a terrorist group in Luton. Members of this group were connected with al-Qaeda, and several of them had been arrested by police in August 2004. At this time the British Secret Service had also kept a close watch on Mohammed Sidique Khan, who might have been part of the Luton group. But they had soon decided that he did not pose a threat.

Developments in the investigation

8 July	Police announce that the death toll is now 49
9 July	Authorities confirm that the three underground blasts took place at the same time
12 July	Police raid three properties in Yorkshire; bomb factory found in Burley, Leeds; hire car found at Luton station
13 July	Police raid a property in Aylesbury; three of the bombers are named
14 July	Nationwide 2-minute silence in memory of the victims
15 July	Magdi Asdi el-Nashar arrested in Cairo in connection with the attacks
17 July	Police release CCTV images of the four bombers at Luton station
18 July	Pakistani government confirms that three of the bombers recently visited Pakistan
19 July	Bombed train carriage removed from tunnel near Edgware Road station

5
The bombs that failed

A state of fear

Nearly two weeks after the explosions, there was still a lot of clearing up to do. The final death toll of 56 was announced on 17 July. London Underground only resumed full services on the Victoria Line and Northern Line on 18 July. Engineers were not able to remove the bombed train carriage from the Edgware Road tunnel until 19 July.

All over the United Kingdom, the security services were on their highest state of alert. They kept a close watch on up to 12 al-Qaeda suspects, with orders that they should shoot to kill anyone they saw carrying a bomb.

There were plenty of reasons to be afraid. During their raids in Leeds, police had discovered a large amount of explosives in a flat in the Burley area. They believed that this was where the rucksack bombs had been made. The **ingredients** for the explosives had probably been mixed together in a bath at the flat. Some of these materials had been found in the boot of the hired car at Luton station. Why had they left it? Did they intend to come back? Were there plans for more bombs?

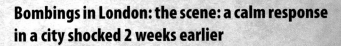

Bombings in London: the scene: a calm response in a city shocked 2 weeks earlier

The *New York Times*, 22 July 2005

Armed police patrolled in train stations all over the country in the days immediately after the bombings.

The second attack

On the morning of Thursday 21 July 2005, Londoners were getting back to their normal way of life. It was two weeks since the bombings had disrupted their lives and brought fear to the streets. Now the tube trains and buses were filling up again. It was also the first day of the Ashes cricket series between England and Australia in north London, which brought extra crowds to the capital.

But at 12:26 p.m. there was an explosion on an Underground train at Shepherd's Bush station on the Hammersmith and City line. Four minutes later, another explosion occurred on a train at Oval station on the Northern Line. At 12:45 p.m. there was a third explosion on a Victoria line train at Warren Street station. Finally, at 1:30 p.m., a device exploded on a number 26 bus on Hackney Road in Bethnal Green.

The explosions were very small and did little damage. Some people near the explosions said that there was a strange smell, like burning rubber, just before the explosions. Eyewitnesses also saw men running away from the scenes of the attacks.

The security operation swung into action again. Many Underground stations were evacuated, and train services on many parts of the system were closed down. Emergency staff arrived at the sites, but soon realized that there was little for them to do. It was clear that the bombs had failed to go off properly. The small bangs had probably been caused by the detonators, not the main explosives.

About two hours after the failed bus bombing, there was another major alert. A man wearing a small rucksack was stopped by police near the Ministry of Defence building in central London. He was forced to lie down before officers handcuffed and arrested him. Another man was later arrested in the Whitehall area, though the Metropolitan Police chief, Ian Blair, said that these arrests were not connected with the earlier explosions.

This number 26 bus was abandoned in east London after one of the explosions.

12:26 p.m.	Small explosion on a train at Shepherd's Bush station
12:30 p.m.	Small explosion on a train at Oval station
12:45 p.m.	Small explosion on a train at Warren Street station
1:30 p.m.	Backpack explodes on a bus in Hackney Road
2:30 p.m.	Police cordon off University College Hospital after reports that a suspected bomber has entered the building
3:30 p.m.	Security alert near Downing Street, Whitehall, where a man is arrested
4:00 p.m.	London police chief says that everything is "firmly under control"

Tragedy in Stockwell

The police force throughout Britain was now in a state of high alert. In London especially, the police were keeping a close watch on anyone who might be involved with extremist groups. On the morning of 22 July, a police team was watching a block of flats in Stockwell, South London. At about 9:30 a.m., a man named Jean Charles de Menezes came out of the flats and made his way to Stockwell station.

Jean Charles de Menezes was 27 years old when he was mistakenly shot dead by police.

COPS SHOOT MAN ON TUBE

The *Sun*, 23 July 2005

Police officers followed him on to the **escalator**. At this point de Menezes ran to get on to a train. He did not know the officers were there, because they were in **plain clothes**. When he was on the train, a policeman grabbed him, while another fired seven bullets into his head. De Menezes died instantly.

It had all been a terrible mistake. De Menezes was a Brazilian electrician who was living and working in London. Police had not identified him properly as a suspect, but followed him simply because he came from the building they were watching. They killed him because they believed he might be carrying a suicide bomb. He was completely innocent.

The tragic killing of Jean Charles de Menezes shocked the nation. It came at a time of high tension, when people were expecting another terrorist attack at any moment. Police with firearms regularly patrolled railway stations and other public places. They also stopped and searched members of the public who looked suspicious to them. Controversially, because three of the bombers had Pakistani backgrounds, most of the people stopped by the police were of Asian origin.

There were complaints about this treatment from the Asian and Muslim communities of Britain. The government tried to find ways of making the situation better. The minister responsible for **counter-terrorism**, Hazel Blears, announced that she would be having eight meetings with Muslim leaders around the country during August.

How the bombings hit business

By 24 July shops, hotels, and other businesses in London were still feeling the effects on their trade:

- shopping: 20% down
- hotels and restaurants: 20% down
- buses: no change
- Underground trains: 450,000 fewer journeys
- cycling: 50,000 more journeys
- London Eye: 25% down
- Tower of London: 25% down
- British Museum: 33% down

6
The arrests begin

The investigation continues

The police now had a big question to answer. Was there a connection between the attacks on 7 July and those on 21 July? They certainly looked similar. In both cases the targets had been three Underground trains and one bus. All the bombs had been carried in rucksacks. Both sets of bombs had also been spread around central London to cover north, south, east, and west.

The four unsuccessful bombers were still at large. However, on 24 July the police found a suspicious package hidden in some bushes at Little Wormwood Scrubs, West London. They made it safe with a **controlled explosion** and then examined it. The device seemed to be a bomb packed inside a plastic food container. It was exactly like the four bombs that had failed to go off three days earlier. This meant that there had not been four bombers, but five.

Police officers carried out a controlled explosion on an item found at Little Wormwood Scrubs.

Naming the suspects

The police were now looking for five men in connection with the 21 July attacks. On 25 July they released the names of two of them. They believed that Yasin Hassan Omar had carried the bomb at Warren Street station, and that Muktar Said Ibrahim had carried the bomb on the bus. Police had already searched Omar's house in north London, where they found a large amount of materials which could have been used to make explosives.

But Omar had already fled the city. On 27 July officers raided two houses in Birmingham and arrested four men. One of them was Yasin Hassan Omar. He fought with police and had to be stunned with an electric shock from a **Taser gun**. He was then driven to Paddington Green police station in London.

The Prevention of Terrorism Act

In March 2005, the British government introduced a new law to deal with the growing threat of terrorist attacks. It was called the Prevention of Terrorism Act 2005. The law allowed the Home Secretary to control people suspected of involvement with terrorism without a full trial in court. Many people were unhappy with the new law and said that it denied people rights which they had enjoyed for more than 700 years.

Under the Act, police could:

• take away a person's passport

• stop them from using the Internet or a mobile phone

• order them to stay inside their homes

• order them to report daily to a police station

• tag them with an electronic device so that their movements could be followed.

This was all part of a massive security campaign. More than 6,000 police officers patrolled the streets in and around London. They arrested and questioned dozens of people under the Prevention of Terrorism Act. Most of these suspects were eventually released without charge.

On Friday 29 July the security services raided a flat in the Peabody Estate in North Kensington. SAS (Special Air Service) soldiers blew off the door with explosives and threw in **tear gas** grenades. The two men inside were ordered to strip and come out with their hands up. They were later named as Ramzi Mohamed (suspected of carrying the Oval bomb) and Muktar Said Ibrahim. At the same time, officers arrested Manfo Kwaku Asiedu in connection with the package found at Little Wormwood Scrubs.

Now four of the suspected bombers were behind bars. Where was the fifth? Officials had tracked Hussain Osman (suspected of carrying the Shepherd's Bush bomb) by **monitoring** his mobile phone calls. These showed that he had left the country and travelled to Italy. Italian police arrested him that evening in Rome.

Italian forensics experts searched this flat in Rome in connection with Hussain Osman.

The suspects are charged

By 8 August, four of the suspected 21 July bombers had been taken to court in London. They were charged with **conspiring** to murder train passengers and with possessing explosives. Ten other men and women faced different charges connected with the attack. Another 28 people had been arrested and later released after questioning.

The police continued checking the evidence. Another breakthough was announced on 20 September. CCTV footage, plus train tickets found in the bombers' houses, showed that three of the 7 July bombers had made a practice run for their deadly journey. Nine days before the bombings they had been filmed at Luton and King's Cross stations. Then they had boarded Underground trains.

On 22 September a police guard brought Hussain Osman back to Britain from Italy on a private aircraft. He was the fifth of the suspected 21 July bombers. The next day Osman was charged with conspiracy to murder and placed in prison with the other four failed bombing suspects.

The London bombings of 2005 were part of a series of savage acts carried out by Islamic extremists throughout the world in this period. Yet the bombers themselves were British, or had lived in Britain for many years. Their families were shocked when they discovered that their relatives were terrorists.

The bomber's final message

"Your democratically elected governments continuously perpetrate atrocities against my people all over the world... Until we feel security you will be our targets, and until you stop the bombing, gassing, imprisonment, and torture of my people we will not stop this fight. We are at war and I am a soldier. Now you too will taste the reality of this situation."

Mohammed Sidique Khan, speaking on a tape broadcast on 1 September 2005, after his death

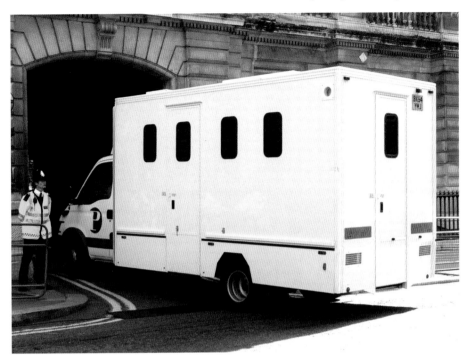

Entire alleged bomb ring held after raids in London and Rome

The *Guardian*, 30 July 2005

It seems that all four of the 7 July bombers had not been extremists for very long. Sidique Khan, for example, had grown up in a non-Muslim area of Leeds and his close friends had been non-Muslims. He had even married a Hindu girl. "He didn't seem interested in Islam," said one friend.

But around 2004 he had joined an Islamic extremist group. There he had met Shehzad Tanweer and Germaine Lindsay. They had watched videos showing the brutal treatment of Muslims in other parts of the world, such as Palestine and Chechnya. These had helped to turn them into radicals. Lindsay's wife said that "his mind had been poisoned" by the group. The result of their experience was the horrifying events of 7 July in London.

Timeline: 7 July

4:00 a.m.	Mohammed Sidique Khan, Hasib Hussain, and Shehzad Tanweer leave Leeds by car
5:00 a.m.	Germaine Lindsay arrives by car at Luton station
6:51 a.m.	The three other bombers arrive at Luton station and join Lindsay. They take a train to King's Cross station, London
8:30 a.m.	The four men get off the train at King's Cross station
8:50 a.m.	Three bombs explode on Underground trains
9:19 a.m.	Police issue terrorist alert; London Underground begins closing down its system
9:35 a.m.	Hasib Hussain boards a number 30 bus outside Euston station
9:47 a.m.	Bomb explodes on bus in Tavistock Square
11:08 a.m.	Bus services in central London shut down
11:10 a.m.	The Metropolitan Police commissioner, Ian Blair, confirms that there are traces of explosives at the sites, showing that this is a terrorist incident

12:05 p.m.	Prime Minister Tony Blair condemns "barbaric" attacks
12:15 p.m.	Little-known group called Secret Organization – al-Qaeda in Europe claims in a website message that it carried out the bombings
3:26 p.m.	The deputy Metropolitan Police chief, Brian Paddick, confirms that police had no warning of the attacks
4:30 p.m.	Services resume on most mainline railways in London
5:30 p.m.	Tony Blair returns to London from Scotland and makes a statement outside 10 Downing Street
6:15 p.m.	Police confirm that at least 37 people have died in the blasts

Timeline: After 7 July

8 July	Police announce that the death toll is now 49; Queen Elizabeth II visits victims in hospital
9 July	London Underground and the Metropolitan Police confirm that the three underground blasts took place at the same time
12 July	Police raid three properties in Leeds and two in Dewsbury; "bomb factory" found in Burley, Leeds; hire car found at Luton station
13 July	Police raid a property in Aylesbury; three of the bombers are named
14 July	Nationwide two-minute silence in memory of the victims
15 July	Magdi Asdi el-Nashar arrested in Cairo in connection with the attacks (he is later released)
17 July	Police release CCTV images of the four bombers at Luton station; death toll confirmed as 56
18 July	Pakistani government confirms that three of the bombers recently visited Pakistan
19 July	Bombed train carriage removed from tunnel near Edgware Road station
21 July	The second attack:
12.26 p.m.	Small explosion on a train at Shepherd's Bush station
12.30 p.m.	Small explosion on a train at Oval station
12.45 p.m.	Small explosion on a train at Warren Street station
1.30 p.m.	A backpack explodes on a bus in Hackney Road

2.30 p.m.	Police cordon off University College Hospital after reports that a suspected bomber has entered the building
3.30 p.m.	Security alert near Downing Street, Whitehall, where a man is arrested
4.00 p.m.	London police chief says that everything is "firmly under control"
22 July	Jean Charles de Menezes, a Brazilian electrician, is mistakenly shot dead by police
23 July	Rucksack bomb found in bushes in Little Wormwood Scrubs, London
25 July	Police name two of the suspected 21 July bombers
26 July	Police find explosives at Hassan Omar's flat in North London
27 July	Police arrest four men in Birmingham in connection with 21 July bombings
29 July	Police arrest three more suspects in North Kensington; Italian police arrest another suspect in Rome
2 August	First of a series of meetings between government ministers and Muslim leaders to improve community relations
4 August	Al-Qaeda spokesman warns of more terrorist attacks on London
6 August	Hassan Omar charged with attempted murder
7 August	Muktar Said Ibrahim and Ramzi Mohamed are charged with attempted murder; Manfu Kwaku Asiedu charged with conspiracy to murder
22 Sept	Hussain Osman charged with attempted murder
8 Dec	Trial date for the five failed bombers set for September 2006

Glossary

alert being ready for attack or danger

asbestos material once used for protecting things from fire and other damage. Its tiny fibres are now known to cause lung disease.

biological agent chemical used in bombs and other weapons, which spreads deadly diseases

CCTV Closed Circuit Television. CCTV cameras are used to record what is happening in streets and other public places

commuter someone who travels regularly from one place to another, usually between home and work

conspire plot or plan an illegal act together in secret

controlled explosion small explosion used by security forces to blow open a door or destroy a suspect package

counter-terrorism campaign aimed at stopping the work of terrorists

detonator device, such as a fuse, which is used to set off an explosion

escalator moving stairway which carries people up and down between the floors of a building

evacuate move people away from an area or building

impact hitting of one thing against another

ingredients materials that are mixed together to make something else

Islam major world religion based on the teachings of the Prophet Mohammed

Islamic extremist someone who promotes Islam in an extreme manner

live rail rail that carries the electricity powering electric trains

monitor watch carefully, or keep track of someone or something

National Grid organization that controls the supply of electricity in the UK

nerve gas gas used in warfare which affects the nerves in the body, causing muscles to stop working normally

Pentagon headquarters of the United States Department of Defense, in Washington

plain clothes police officers dressed in ordinary clothes instead of uniforms so that they look like civilians

power surge sudden increase in the strength of the electricity supply, which can cause damage

Qu'ran (or Koran) main sacred Islamic text

refrigerated truck vehicle fitted with a compartment that can be kept very cold

rush hour period in the early morning or late afternoon when most people are travelling to or from work

security camera see CCTV camera

security curtain plastic sheeting hung over the entrance to the scene of a crime to keep out members of the public

suicide bomber terrorist who kills himself or herself and others by detonating explosives which he or she is carrying

Taser gun gun which stuns someone by releasing a powerful electric shock

tear gas gas released by a grenade, which irritates a person's eyes and other senses and makes them helpless

terrorist someone who uses violence and terror to promote his or her political or religious beliefs

Finding out more

Books

Beyond the Front Lines: How the News Media Cover a World Shaped by War,
Philip Seib (Palgrave Macmillan, 2004)

Conspiracy Theories: Real-life Stories of Paranoia, Secrecy and Intrigue,
David Southwell and Sean Twist (Carlton, 2004)

Just The Facts: Terrorism,
Richard Dingley (Heinemann Library, 2003)

The Middle East: The Making of the Middle East,
David Downing (Raintree, 2006)

Secret Soldiers: Special Forces in the War Against Terrorism,
Peter Harclerode (Cassell, 2002)

Snapshots in History: September 11 – Attack on America,
Andrew Langley (Compass Point, 2006)

Terrorism: The Impact On Our Lives,
Alex Woolf (Hodder Wayland, 2005)

Troubled World: The War Against Terrorism,
David Downing (Heinemann Library, 2003)

Witness to History: September 11, 2001,
Sean Connolly (Heinemann Library, 2003)

Websites

news.bbc.co.uk

> Search for "London bombings" for BBC news reports, pictures, and interviews

www.redcross.org.uk

> The Red Cross helped to rescue people caught up in the bombings. Find out more about what they do through their website.

www.london.gov.uk

> The website of the Mayor of London helps you keep up with events in the capital.

www.september11news.com

> Includes a complete timeline of events before, during, and after 11 September 2001, together with a directory of images and news articles

Further research

If you are interested in finding out more about the London bombings, try researching the following topics:

- the Madrid and Bali bombings

- the war on terror

- Al–Qaeda

Index